SLOIG ON THE SOSH!

AN ECCENTRIC LOOK AT SUFFOLK

CHARLIE HAYLOCK

With cartoons by Barrie Appleby

COUNTRYSIDE BOOKS
NEWBURY BERKSHIRE

First published 2012
© Charlie Haylock 2012

COUNTRYSIDE BOOKS
3 Catherine Road
Newbury, Berkshire

To view our complete range of books,
please visit us at
www.countrysidebooks.co.uk

ISBN 978 1 84674 308 5

To Peter Coleman

Designed by Peter Davies, Nautilus Design
Produced through MRM Associates Ltd., Reading
Printed by Berforts Information Press Ltd,
Oxford

CONTENTS

ACKNOWLEDGEMENTS

I would like to thank the following people, organisations, societies, associations and companies for helping me in my research for this book on Suffolk. Without their input this book would never have been written. A special thank you goes to Lesley Dolphin, BBC Radio Suffolk and BBC Radio Suffolk's listeners.

R. J. Alecock
T. G. Alecock
W. Alecock McMahon
Barrie Appleby
BBC Radio Suffolk
BBC Radio Suffolk's Listeners
Sylvia Bickers
Alice Catchpole
Kim Catchpole
Neil Catchpole
Simon Clegg
Coddenham Village History Club
Peter Coleman
Lesley Dolphin
Gavin Downes
Dave Feaviour
Janice Feller
Doug Feveyear
Gainsborough's House Society
Gale
Rex Garrod
Sally Garrod
Pat Godbold
Grimwood Family, Boxford
Steve Harvey
Bill Haylock

Ipswich Town FC
Maggie James
Nick Jenkins
Peter Jones
Jerv Jordan
Louise Kennedy
Tim & Sarah Kindred
Mick Kerry
Vivienne Leeder
Sue Lodwick
Heather Marshall
Bruce Martin
Jo Miles
Aaron Moss
St Edmundsbury Borough Council
            Heritage Service
Suffolk Record Office, Ipswich
Suffolk Record Office, B.S.E.
The Jerv Jordan Collection
The Suffolk Punch Trust
The Yellow House
Margaret Thompson
Dominic Wall
Heather Welch
Windmill House Collection
Rosemary Woodward

FOREWORD

Two 'Hossmen' at Barrow Hall c. 1890.
(Suffolk Record Office, Ipswich –ref K681/1/27/2)

The popularity of 'Haylock's Half Hour for Forty Minutes', on BBC Radio Suffolk every Thursday afternoon, with me and Lesley Dolphin, was quite overwhelming. Listener participation was remarkable, and many requests just poured in.

The seed was set for *Sloightly on the Sosh! – An Eccentric Look at Suffolk.*

Thank yer koindly tew yew awl t'gether!

The theme of this extended half hour started with an A to Z of Suffolk surnames. Each week we are gradually working our way through the alphabet, with names that were first registered in Suffolk and historically located only in Suffolk. The meaning of each surname and its derivation are discussed in turn; the vast majority being of Anglo-Saxon origin, with a few Normans slung in for good measure, plus a few Vikings here and there and other odds and bobs.

Listeners were also invited to contact the show if they wanted to know more about their particular surnames, what they meant and whether they were principally Suffolk or not. The response was fantastic, so much so, that Lesley Dolphin suggested the idea of another Charlie Haylock book which would incorporate a chapter on Suffolk surnames. I *lissened* to what Lesley had to say. Nowhere, through all my research, have I found a book or dictionary, dedicated to Suffolk surnames.

Well, there is now! This has become a first! And the middle chapter of *Sloightly on the Sosh!*, is just that, and simply titled, 'Suffolk Surnames'.

The other chapters in *Sloightly on the Sosh!*, are Suffolk at its best. But why the title? The phrase is used by many an *owd* Suffolker, and literally means that *suffen* is not quite straight and perhaps is very apt and fitting for my *Eccentric Look at Suffolk.* Once again, I'm very fortunate to have Barrie Appleby, the internationally-famed cartoonist, to endorse this eccentricity.

The term 'on the sosh', according to John Cuming Walters in *Bygone Suffolk*, was used extensively in the Suffolk flint mining industry when cutting a shaft downwards and across to get to the next seam of flint. Also, Bob Malster, who wrote *The Mardler's Companion to East Anglian Dialect*, said in an interview with Nick Jenkins, radio producer, that the Brandon flint miners had a technique of excavating flint, which they called *bubbahutch'n on the sosh!* And Claxton's glossary of Suffolk words and phrases, refers to 'on the sosh' as crooked and slanting, and further goes on to say that a nail driven in aslant would be 'sosh wise'.

Howsumever, this eccentric look at Suffolk, in places, will take you into parts of Suffolk social history in a way that's never ever been seen afore. Perhaps you will see why I have been given the nickname, 'The Hysterical Historian'. All the facts I give are genuine and true, and backed up by years and years of research and study. I suppose it's the way I deliver it *accrorst*,

Miss Joan Wheat standing outside Pump Farm, Assington.
(The Jerv Jordan Collection)

and why my CD, *The Confessions of an Hysterical Historian* was a best seller, and a part of the *Suffolk Voices* Series.

I enjoyed writing the chapter, 'Suffolk Norfolk Banter', as it brought back fond memories of the many times I have visited Norfolk, and is also a Suffolk tribute to numerous friends I have from north of the Waveney in the only way I know how.

The hilarious chapter, 'Inside Toilet Outside', is truly a *duzzy* look at Suffolk social history, and portrays Barrie Appleby at his absolute best. It also reminds me of how times used to be – thank goodness – in days gone by. Was it really like that? Yes, it was! It will bring back memories to some of you, and total disbelief to others.

'Suffolk Squit' at its best and funniest, is *squit*, in the true Suffolk tradition. *Howsumever*, if it's just nonsense, then it's also *squit*, (but said differently). So if you tell me it's *squit*, then I thank you kindly but if you tell me it's *squit*, then I'll understand.

I suppose what I'm really trying to say is that, in these times of severe cut backs and economic hardship, with newspapers full of doom and gloom, I'm trying to bring some laughter and joy into the situation, and to put smiles on faces. I try to do it through my one-man shows and talks, in the village halls, theatres, community centres and various other venues. I also bring this eccentricity into my after-dinner speaking. Hopefully I've done the same in *Sloightly on the Sosh!*

I hope you agree and enjoy reading this book *t'gether* and, at the same time, learn some genuine, interesting and intriguing facts about Suffolk.

Charlie Haylock

CHAPTER 1

Suffolk Norfolk Banter

Peter Coleman. (courtesy of Mick Kerry, Stowupland.)

As you will have noticed, this book has been dedicated to a great friend of mine, Peter Coleman. It is worth noting, that if it hadn't have been for Peter Coleman ....there wouldn't be a Charlie Haylock today..........and that's a fact!

There was I, doing my funny little turns and telling yarns in the folk sessions and clubs of East Anglia. I got to know Peter very well, especially at our regular visits to the music sessions at the Low House, Laxfield, every Tuesday afternoon. Peter took me to one side and gave me some advice about what I was doing, and how I ought to change direction. I took his advice and the rest is history. *Cood Blaast!* I've got to sit down! I feel a bit dizzy. Don't worry! I'll be all right ... just need to settle down ... have cuppa tea and take a few deep breaths ... That's better! ...That was close!

What's going on you say? Well, some of you won't believe this; but I've actually publicly acknowledged and thanked a man from Norfolk ... and dedicated this here book to him!

Seriously though – *Thank yer koindly Peter!*

It's fair to say, that the Suffolk Norfolk banter, (Norfolk Suffolk banter if you are from north of the Waveney), has been going *fairly* for hundreds of years, and is still going strong.

Make no mistake, Suffolk dish it out to Norfolk to get it back, and likewise the opposite is true, except Suffolk is better at it than Norfolk, (here we go ... already started). The one golden rule in this cross county banter, is that

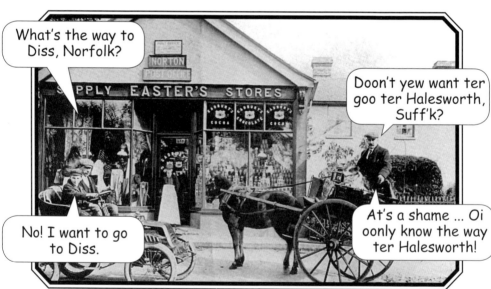

(Suffolk Record Office, Ipswich – ref K681/1/340/3)

you keep a straight face throughout. First one who smiles or laughs is out. It's also fair to say, that once these kindly insults are delivered, then it's most disappointing if a retort is not forthcoming, and one can quite easily lose respect if a reply is not readily at hand. It's natural to have this to-ing and fro-ing, and it is good humoured, but the dead pan face makes it difficult for the *furrener* to comprehend and understand. Understandable, I suppose. But I do have some wonderful illustrations and examples.

Lowestoft Book Signing Session

I was doing a book signing session in a Lowestoft bookshop, and there was quite a queue, with their books already opened for my message and scrawl. Then all of a sudden, a book was plonked on the table, and a broad Norfolk accent says, 'Ken yew soign ut please Chaarlie?'. Straight away I asked him if it had been a bit heady coming across the Waveney. The reply involved needing his passport stamped coming into Suffolk, and that he was on a strict timetable, as he didn't want to get too infected. This banter went on for a minute or two, and the queue were thoroughly enjoying it. Then suddenly, out of the blue, a voice boomed out, 'Cor blimey! Don't you two carry on t'gevver!

Before I could respond, my Norfolk opponent nipped in first, (not often that happens ... letting Norfolk get in first), and said, 'Doon't yew hev a goo at Chaarlie ... he's a good owd booy is Chaarlie!'

'Old on mate ! You're 'avin' a larf aintcha! You've just bin 'avin' a go at 'im!'

The Norfolk reply was invaluable, 'This hare is Norf'k Suff'k roivalry. Yew jest doon't understand. This has bin goo'n on for hundreds a yares. Best yew bugger roff 'n' leave us tew ut!' The queue responded and said, 'Yes!' and started clapping. The interfering stranger sloped off with his tail between his legs.

My Norfolk opponent turned towards me saying, 'At shew 'em bor,' shook me by the hand and wished me well as he left. And the book signing continued ...

Norfolk W.I.

I had occasion to give an afternoon talk to a W.I group meeting near Woodbastwick, some 7 miles north-east of Norwich, two weeks after Norwich City had been promoted to the Premiership. Now, I honestly thought that I wouldn't get too much banter from these lovely ladies, especially about football. How wrong can you get.

I arrived, and being the only bloke, straight away I was approached by a very regal lady who quite simply said, 'Mister Haylock ?'

I half nodded and replied, 'Yes'.

'From Suffolk?'

Again I replied, 'Yes'

'Oi suppoose yew were raather pleased ter hare that Norwich City got promooted ter the Premiership? ... But then aggen ... Oi suppoose yew're an Ipsidge Town supporter?'

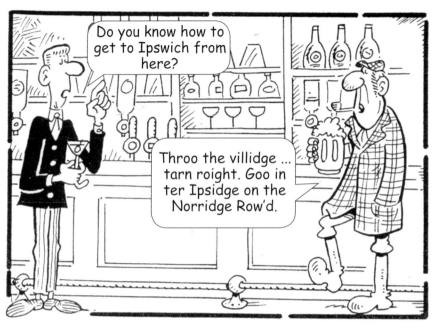

It had started the moment I had walked through the door ... but it hadn't finished.

I had set myself up on the stage ready for my afternoon talk, and Lady President had set her table up, just below the stage. She whipped through the W.I. business in about fifteen minutes flat. Then she came out with a pearler. 'Ladies! About ar guest speaker. Mister Haylock. All Oi'll say is ... he's an Ipsidge Town supporter! ... Ladies! ... Mister Haylock!' and then sat down.

I quickly looked at the audience amidst the clapping and everyone was smiling except five people – I knew they were not from East Anglia!

I slowly stood there and looked. There was silence. I waited for as long as I dare without saying a word. 'Good afternoon ladies!' – and a hearty response was heard. I started my talk, 'As an Ipsidge Town supporter, Oi would loike to congratulate City on being promoted to the Premiership. Oi have found owt t'day that Lady President has been a loife long supporter of Norridge City, and has been a season tick't holder ever since she was a young gal of fourtee'n'... Hope yew enjoyed moy talk!' and I turned to walk off stage.

Everyone laughingly knew ... and I returned to the stage and we had a fantastic afternoon. But it didn't finish there. Some days later, I received the most wonderful and sincere thank you card from Lady President – one that I have treasured.

Norfolk Rotary

Once again, I had the occasion to visit Norfolk. This time to a 50th Charter Night for a Rotary evening, right in the heart of this East Anglian county, (don't like saying Norfolk too often). They had even started afore I got there. The menu and details of the evening were all superbly done for this auspicious occasion, in lovely scroll writing, including the three guest speakers. The local MP was first speaker, another local dignitary next, and then me. But what had they *writ* down to introduce me? 'Words of Wisdom by Charlie Haylock, a Suffolk Lad'. I knew what was coming ... so I nipped in first when it was my turn.

Eventually I was introduced. I again slowly stood there and waited, and waited. 'Even'n !' I said, and once again, a goodly response. Then I read it out, 'Words of Wisdom by Charlie Haylock – a Suffolk lad'. Immediately from two points in the audience came what I had expected, 'Foind that hard won't yer bor!', and 'Words of wisdom? You'll foind 'at difficult booy'.

'Yes, Oi did' was my reply. 'Oi fow'nd ut very difficult .... to know how

Drawing by Gale; characters by Barrie Appleby.

simple to make ut for a Norfolk audience t'understand!'

The audience laughed and were now ready, and once again, a superb evening.

Beccles Family Tree

I gave a talk on the Suffolk dialect, and its importance in the evolution of spoken English, to a group of local historians in Beccles. This also included looking at the evolution of English surnames, especially Suffolk surnames.

After the talk, I was approached by two older East Anglians, both the best of friends. One was born and bred from just north of the Waveney, and the other from just south of this great divide. The Suffolk Norfolk banter between them was second to none, and one knew instinctively, not to join in.

The Suffolk side of this duo was rather proud to tell me about his rather rare Suffolk surname, and that he had started researching his family tree. He said that it had been quite easy and straight forward, until he got to great grandad. Then he said that it started to get a bit difficult, and that the tree started to wander around somewhat.

Immediately the Norfolk friend stated,

'That be 'bout the toime the boike was invented', and he kept a very straight face.

The Suffolk response was quite simple, yet very effective,

'Yeah. T'is trew. But moind yew ... he din't coycle accrorst the bridge!'

'Cood blaast! 'at would a made ut even more difficult ter trace 'em awl!'

They then wandered off, still prattling on, the best of friends. Wonderful!

History of Suffolk lecture in Stowmarket

There I was, explaining how Suffolk had evolved and her history. I talked about the Romans leaving these pleasant shores, and then started to wax lyrical about our direct ancestors, the Angles, and how they invaded and settled. How they first arrived on the East Coast, being led by an Angle chieftain called Yipps, (or *suffen* very similar), and how they built the first Angle settlement, and how it became known as Yippswiche, (later of course, to become Ipswich).

I then explained that some of the Angles spread across the country due west, and that others had gone due north and settled in what is now present day Norfolk, and some stayed behind, in what is now called Suffolk.

Immediately from the audience, a Norfolk voice was heard saying rather proudly,

'That must make us the Right Angles then!'

'More loike the Obtruse Angles!' came a quick Suffolk retort.

'So those left behind must be Cute Angles! Mmmmm!' was the Norfolk response.

'No, deeyer booy', came the Suffolk reply in somewhat of a deeper voice, 'We're the Straight Angles!'

I nipped in quick, saying, 'Whether we loike ut or not, that does make us Adjacent Angles t'gether,' and carried on with my lecture.

During the interval, these two protagonists looked for one another and, once found, shook hands and then had an amiable chat over a cuppa tea.

Hopefully these have been true examples of how the rivalry and the banter still continues between these two magnificent counties today. How, underneath those dead pan faces, there is enjoyment and a healthy respect for each other. We love one another really but please don't let on and tell 'em. That would go and spoil it all together ... can't tell a Norfolk man that we love him! Cood Blaast! No!

Hopefully, too, you found this chapter to have been a totally unbiased and well-balanced account of Suffolk Norfolk banter, treating each splendid, ancient and historic county the same but heavily weighted *t'wards* Suffolk! ... **of course**

CHAPTER 2

The Differing Suffolk Dialects

We talk about the Suffolk dialect as if there is just the one dialect. There isn't. There are several – the best part of a fair few, as we say. *Furreners* say that the North Suffolk dialect sounds like South Norfolk. I'd like to put it another way. South Norfolk sounds like North Suffolk – that's the right way round. They also say that North Essex and South Suffolk are similar, and they are.

But the North Essex and South Norfolk dialects are miles apart – literally. So, therefore, as we travel through Suffolk, the dialect gradually changes from North Essex to South Norfolk. This change is quite distinct.

Percy Edwards, as some of you will remember, was a fantastic bird and animal impersonator in the second half of the 20th century. He had a fantastic ear. So much so, that when Percy, as a celebrity, did his hospital visits and tours, he took great pride in recognising the various Suffolk dialects.

Percy Edwards could tell what Suffolk town or village you came from, within hearing just a few words.......a couple of sentences at the most.

'Morn'n Perrsy. Hower yoo t'day ber?' came a voice from a bed in Primrose Ward.

'Morn'n ... from Sudbury then', Percy would proudly say. And he'd be right. He'd have a kindly chat and move on.

'Morn'n Parrsy. Hower yoo t'day buh?' came another voice from the next bed, and straight away Percy would recognise it as a Bury St Edmunds dialect.

Every town and village is that little bit different as you move across Suffolk, and so it gradually changes into quite different dialects on the extreme edges of the county.

Bor

A best part of a tidily sum of Suffolkers, reckon that this little word is the Suffolk way of saying, 'booy', well, it isn't. The Suffolk way of saying 'booy', and you might not believe this ... is ... 'booy'! Bor is pure Anglo-Saxon for a male friend, and everyone in the country uses it in one particular word. I shall explain ...

We do not say in Suffolk that it's nearly six o'clock, we say, 'It's nigh on six o'clock'. We don't say, 'There's close on twenty prizes in the raffle', we say that there's nigh on twenty prizes. And, of course, 'The end is nigh!' The word 'nigh' means 'close to', 'nearby' and 'nearly'. Therefore, if we have a male friend, 'bor', living next door or opposite ... he becomes our 'nigh bor'. Yes, and that's how we get the English word 'neighbour'. So when a Scotsman, or Welshman, or Australian, or American or whoever, (including Norfolk), says, 'Neighbour', (pronounced nayber), that little *ber* on the end is just the same way as some of us good *owd* Suffolkers saying it too.

But, how this little word, 'bor', changes throughout the county. In the Sudbury area it's pronounced 'ber', and by the time you get to Bury St

Oi ken tell she come fr'm Glemsf't ... 'n' she hent even said a wud!

Percy Edwards at the Glemsford Fête c.1966
(The Jerv Jordan Collection)

Edmunds, it becomes 'buh'. When you get to Stowmarket, it's now pronounced as 'bo', (as in bomb without the *mb*). Now on to Leiston, where we hear it as 'bor', and then Lowestoft, when it becomes 'boor' (Norfolk appears to have copied the latter pronunciation). This is just one big example, of how just one little word greatly changes.

Make, Cake, Snape, etc

The 'ay' sound in Suffolk, as in make, (mayke), cake, (cayke), Snape, (Snaype) etc, etc, has taken over, even in north Suffolk. But, in the north of the county, some of the older generation are still using the 'air' sound, making it *mairk* and *cairk* for 'make' and 'cake', as it used to be in Elizabethan times. My father who was brought up in Snape always referred to it as *Snairp*. We also get this being pronounced as an 'er' sound, and you will see this particular example at the end of this chapter. It is a wonderful humorous poem *writ* by Elizabeth Davey from Halesworth, as she passed the age of seventy. The beauty of this poem, is that she's *writ* it in an old Halesworth dialect.

Enow and Hoss Trow

Once again, you'll see an example of this in Elizabeth's poem, about the trials and tribulations of getting old. She uses the word *enow* for 'enough'. This was common in north and mid Suffolk, and my Grandfather always said *hoss trow* for 'horse trough'. Making the 'ough' into an 'ow' sound is a Viking pronunciation and just shows how the Suffolk dialect was influenced

(Coddenham History Club)

somewhat by the Danes when they invaded Angle territory all those years ago. I'm rather glad it doesn't apply to all 'ough' words. I can't imagine going to the doctors with a tickley cow, or even a hooping cow, and then having to go to the chemist and asking to be given some cow mixture.

The Suffolk Double Syllables, (but not all of Suffolk)

Why does East Suffolk tend to talk a lot quicker than West Suffolk? It's because of the double syllables. West Suffolk elongate a great number of words in their vocabulary.

Heeyer in S.W. Suffolk, *hare* in N.E. Suffolk and 'here' in the Oxford English Dictionary; *Deeyer* and *dare* for 'dear'; *Jew'n* and *Joon* for 'June'; *feey'd* for 'feed', and *indeey'd* for 'indeed'; *foiy've* and *foive* for 'five'; *dow'un tow'un,*

(Courtesy of Ipswich Town F.C.)

for 'down town'. The list is endless but it does make the dialect of this particular area more sing songy. And there's the classic case when a very West Suffolk Miss Bone went to the doctors for her nine o'clock appointment. The receptionist was new and from *furren* parts (London, I think), and could not find Miss Bowen's notes anywhere.

Howsumever, this is not just a West/East divide. You cannot draw straight lines when it comes to dialects … there's too much overlapping in different directions. In the heart of East Suffolk, with just its smattering of double syllables, there is Ipswich. And Ipswich is very much like the west of the county, with its profusion of double syllables. A little oasis … well … praps not so little. And at Portman *Row'ad*, you'll hear the familiar chant of 'Up The Tow'un!'

Southern Football League – February 5th 1938.
Ipswich Town 3 – Colchester United 2.
Attendance 23,449.

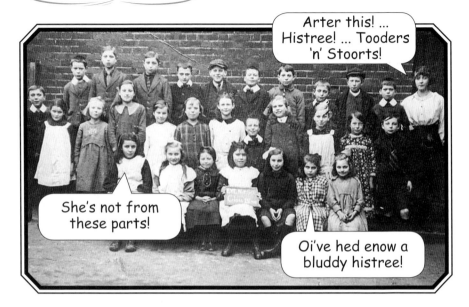

(Suffolk Record Office, Ipswich – ref K681/1/153/26)

The Oos and the Ewes

There is a tendency for west and south Suffolk to pronounce the 'u' in computer as *compewter* and east and north Suffolk as *compooter*. The same in t*ribewnal* and *triboonal* for 'tribunal' and, of course, at school we studied either the *Tewders* and *Stewarts* or the *Tooders* and *Stoorts*, but Tudors and Stuarts at the Royal Hospital School at Holbrook.

Other Words

North Suffolk cricketers would shout, *Hull ut oover hare bor*!, if they wanted the cricket ball. South Suffolkers would shout, *Hoss ut over heeyer ber*!. The word 'hull' for throw tends to be mid to north of the county and very rarely used south of that. The use of the word 'hoss' for 'throw', likewise is limited to the south. *Howsumever*, both would use *hoss* when gulping food down – *Cood blaast, he hully hossed ut dow'un* – and, of course, both would use *hoss* when referring to an *owd hoss*.

South Suffolkers also tend to use the word 'ho' for 'no', but only at the beginning of the sentence and usually in answer to a question, when an emphasis has to be made.

Suffolk Record Office. Ipswich ref K681/1/153/23

Arter Seventy – In Suffolk

Oi've hed me three score year an' ten,
An' um gorn downhill roite fast:
Um owder tha Oi've ever bin,
Spuz Oi worn't meant ter last.

Thas a grut owd hump come on me back,
Me ligs are gitt'n bandy:
Oi fare ter zig-zag orf the track -
A zimmer would come handy.

Oi puff and pant loike an owd steam train
When Oi sarnick up the hills:
Then Oi remember once agin -
Oi hint took me warter pills.

If me hear'n aid's tarned up ter hoigh
It merks a duzzy din,
Yit when it's tarned down low, Oh moy!
It moight not as well be in.

Me oyesoight too is nearly gorn,
They say one's betta than the t'other.
When Oi hint got me glasses on,
Wuds run inter one another.

Oi het ter keep me hid a-covered,
Me hair's a hully gitt'n thin.
But Oi ent nun too bothered,
Thas enow grow on me chin.

Oi troied to chaw a bit a meat,
But found that Oi worn't eble.
No wonder Oi wuz nearly beat -
Me teeth wuz on the teble.

Still Oi spuz Oi marn't merk a fuss.
Thas fooks warse off than me.
But Oi orfen hev a swear un cuss.
Cos the warst is yit ter be!

Elizabeth Davey 1993

CHAPTER 3

Inside Toilet Outside

(A look into the Suffolk social history you won't be *larnt* at school)

My Aunt Hilda's Four-Seater (And we are not talking motor cars!)

I called in at my Aunt Hilda's one day, and she say to me, 'Charlie! Put the kettle on for a cuppa tea. Oi've jest gotta goo t' the toilet.' Well, I put the kettle on and a little while later my aunt came back, and she say to me, 'Cood blast, booy! Oi remember, when Oi was a little owd gal in Edwardst'n – we never hed an insoide toilet, we hed a privy down the bottom a the garden, an' 'at wuz a four seater,' she say.

My aunt then went on to explain how it all worked: there were two large seats for mum and dad and two small seats for the children with no partitions – all in there together! There were seven children, and Mum and Dad made nine *on* 'em. And in the morning, when they were all going off to work or school, they'd all be lined up waiting to go to the toilet. Dad would come out the privy and one of the teenagers would go in. A *little 'un* comes out and another *young 'un* goes in. Mum comes out and another teenager goes in, and so it would go on. Aunt Hilda then made one of her telling asides, 'You din't want ter be laast !' she say.

I was giving a talk some time ago, to one of the many W.I. group meetings I'm invited to, and I was halfway through explaining about my Aunt Hilda's four seater, when two ladies at the front interrupted quite loudly saying, 'No! No! This isn't true!' Then, all of a sudden, from the back of the packed hall, a lady in her eighties shouts out, in a broad Suffolk accent, 'Thas Roight! We did. We hed a two seater dow'n the bott'm a our gaard'n. 'An when Oi went down there in the morn'n 'at wuz the long'st conversation Oi hed with moy husb'nd all day!' She brought the house down and everyone there, in that hall, then knew this was real social history and not made up. *Howsumever*, on with the story ...

A Double Shared (... is not a double halved!)

After I'd finished my cuppa with Aunt Hilda, I was driving home and I passed my ancient parents' house, (both aged 88 each). I called in, just to check to see how they were getting on and, of course, I tell them what Aunt Hilda say to me earlier on. Well! The response I got from my father was nothing short of astounding. He say to me, 'Caw'd a Hell booy! 'At's nuth'n! When Oi wuz a booy in Snairpe, we hed a two seater dow'n the bott'm a our gaard'n an' we shared ut with the person next door – an 80 year *owd* spinster called Miss Pargetter!'

Dad then went on to explain that every morning when he went to school, he'd run down to the double at the bottom of the garden, go in, and she'd already be in there. Every school day and Saturday morning, they'd be in there together but never on a Sunday. Miss Pargetter was a c*huchgoer* and Dad was a *meetiner*. So he was in there earlier afore he went off to chapel somewhere in Aldeburgh which, obviously, was a lot further away than Snape church.

Finningham V.C.P. School 1959
(Suffolk Record Office, Ipswich; ref – K681/2/86/17)

We can all imagine a six year *owd* boy going off to school in Snape in 1920. But can we imagine what an 80 year *owd* spinster looked like in 1920? She didn't have a skirt that went down to the knee – it went all the way down to the ankles – not the skimpy things I see hanging on the line today ... that was a pair of frilly bloomers that also went all the way to the ankles ... then on top of that ... a whole load of petticoats ... that's fair to say ... that she has so much on ... she didn't have time to take them off. So, if you look in the history books, you'll see that lots of these long-legged frilly bloomers were either open-crotched or open-legged (you had to be careful!).

Can you imagine what that must have been like? The two of them sitting there holding a conversation together doing their bodily functions.

Dad also told me that one day he pulled off a few sheets of squared off newspaper to use accordingly, and Miss Pargetter quite calmly said, 'Tubal, hev yew read what's happen'n in Saxmund'm?'

I told you this was social history you won't be *larnt* at school! *Howsumever*. the story continues ...

Uncle Charlie's New Insoide Toilet Outsoide

After I heard these two fascinating scatological tales, I thought I would do some research. I found out that Uncle Charlie was the first person in the village to have an inside toilet outside. This is very logical to the Suffolker. You cannot have an outside toilet inside the house, but you can have an inside toilet outside. Wouldn't be right otherwise!

You go out of your back door, go a few paces right or left and there it is – usually adjoined to the kitchen, normally with a blue door, about a foot from the ground and zig zag all along the top. There was no lock on the door because there was a diamond-shape cut out, which was used for looking through to see if anyone was in there – 'Oops! Sorry! Din't realoise yew were in 'ere! Oi'll come back when yew've finish'd!'

Once again I was explaining this to a W.I meeting with a difference. They had brought their husbands along. Yes! And when I spoke about looking through the diamond, there was just a little bit more laughter from a certain section of the audience. Straightaway, I knew! I pointed to the laughing couple and said to the gentleman, 'Yew looked through that diamond! Din't yer booy?' But afore he could answer, his wife shouted back, 'Yes he did! Thas how we met!' ... (It doesn't bare thinking about!)

Well, Uncle Charlie went down the local pub and met up with his *owd*

mate Duggy Deakins. 'Well, Charlie, moy deeyer booy! What's 'at new insoide toilet outsoide loike 'en bor?' was the immediate question.

'Well, Oi come out moy back door ... no more do Oi hev to goo dow'n the bott'm a the gaard'n ... Oi goo a few paces ... sit dow'n ... do the business ... wipe moy ... .pull the chain 'an 'at flush ut all away. Don't know where ut goo to .... but 'at goo somewhere.'

'Caw'd a hell !' say Duggy, 'Thas suffen good!'

'Ar! But you'll never guess what else 'at's got bor', retorts Uncle Charlie.

'What hev 'at got 'en booy?' enquires Duggy.

Uncle Charlie's reply was sincere, 'Thas got a toilet roll 'n' toilet paper!'

'What'll yew dew with awl your newspapers now?' asked Duggy, wandering away.

(The Jerv Jordan Collection)

Side section of outside toilet by Aaron Moss.
Cartoon characters by Barrie Appleby

33

(Suffolk Record Office, Ipswich – Ref K681/2/80/25)

The Difference Between a 'Holer' and a 'Seater'

There is a big difference! Generally, the one holer was a bar, underneath which was a hole – a deep hole, (and possibly two holes for the two-holer, and three, etc, etc). When the holes were full up, they would then be dug out. This was normally done at night-time to avoid stinking out the neighbourhood. The contents were loaded onto a cart, lovingly referred to as the 'lavender' or 'honey' cart, (nobody wanted to say s**t cart). And it is fair to say, that in lots of cases, the contents were then generously spread on the garden or the allotment. No need for artificial fertilisers in *them* days!

The seater was more refined. It was normally a wooden bench with an appropriate sized hole, and a round wooden cover with a handle. Inside the bench, below the hole, would be a large bucket and when full, would be taken away. The contents were then thrown away (sometimes referred to as the 'buck't and chuck't') and, as with the *holer*, very often on the garden or allotment.

'The Fust Toime Oi Got the Cane'

An *owd* Suffolker's account of days at school

We had two outside toilets at school, the 'Boys' at one end of the school, and the 'Girls' at the *t'other* end. The 'Boys' was quite a simple affair, with a black-painted wall and a gulley at the bottom, *sloightly on the sosh*, so it would all drain away. There was also the 'little room', which had a wooden bench with a hole in it, and the bucket was underneath. There was also a round wooden cover to place over the hole, when not in use. At the back of this little room was a small door, with a wing nut to keep it shut. This access was used by the caretaker in order to take out the full bucket and empty it somewhere – on the allotment, I think!

The 'Girls' had two 'little rooms' joined together, and obviously had two small doors round the back.

Well, me and a mate of mine used to creep round the back of the 'Girls' and undo the wing nut, and open the door slightly. We would have a stick with a feather tied on the end and we waited. And when one of the *gals* sat down, we opened the door a little more and 'tickled their arse with a feather'.

Whilst this was great fun for us, we still wanted to be a bit more adventurous. So one time we were armed, not with a tickle feather, but with some stinging nettles ... Yes!

We waited a while and then our chance came. My mate opened the small door a little wider and I carefully put my hand in, clutching the nettles, and jabbed just at the right moment. *Bullseye! Yes! Cood blaast she hully shrik!*

Howsumever, at the same time as there was an almighty yell and scream coming from the 'Girls', a very firm hand was placed on my shoulder. It was the teacher! Me and my mate were both marched down to the Headmaster, (by the ears), and had to wait outside his office. We had to wait whilst she was in there telling him what had happened. The wait seemed ages and ages, and we got even more scared as the waiting continued. It was all done deliberate to make us suffer. Then the dreaded sound – a deep booming voice was heard – 'Come in here, boys! Now!'

'Caught in the act, eh?' he growled.

'It wuz the fust toime we done ut sir.', I replied.

'No excuse!' shouted the Headmaster, 'Bend over! Now!'

And he made us wait in this position as he went to the cane cupboard, selected which one was required, and then came back. We were waiting but he made us wait even more; he had *suffen* to say.

'So you think it funny, do you, making young girls scream?' he growled. 'Better give you a taste of your own medicine then!'

'Y – y– yes sir!', was our feeble reply.

'Yes!' he boomed, 'Yes, now you will find out what it's like to have your arse stung!'

Six of the best, we both got, and then told to go, as the Headmaster pointed to the door.

'We dint scream! But cood blaast – our arses hully stung!'

And you'll be pleased to hear that we never did it again.

Drawing by Gale. Characters by Barrie Appleby.

Drawing by Gale

I hope you enjoyed this chapter together, this nonsensical, yet very accurate observation in Suffolk social history. If only we were *larnt* this at school!

CHAPTER 4

Famous Owd Suffolkers

Suffolk has tended to keep itself to itself and, as a result, is not generally known for having very many notorious and famous people – but, yes, we do! In this chapter I'm going to give a mention to just two of them, and *a couple a three* of them in the next book..

Thomas Gainsborough

'At awl start'd, one noight, ... when Oi paint'd the tow'un red!

Portrait of Thomas Gainsborough
(By kind permission of Gainsborough's House Society)

Gainsborough's Mrs Mary Cobbold with her daughter Anne, c1752
(By kind permission of Gainsborough's House Society)

Thomas was born in Sudbury, in 1727 to a well-to-do clothier. At an early age he *shew* an aptitude for drawing, and was supported and encouraged by his parents, especially his mother, who herself was of an artistic nature and excelled in the painting of flowers. There are also stories of Thomas bunking off lessons (and they talk about kids today!), from Sudbury Grammar School, so he could follow his passion for art, doing drawings of the surrounding countryside. At the age of thirteen, he was sent to London to study and be trained by Hubert Gravelot and Francis Hayman. The first was an engraver and draughtsman, and the other, a landscape artist and illustrator. Both would give him a good grounding that would lay the foundation for a brilliant career.

Gainsborough married Margaret Burr in 1746, rather hurriedly, but unfortunately the young child died. Three years later they moved from London to Sudbury, where they began to raise a family and stayed till 1752. They moved to Ipswich after Thomas had felt he had painted all that he could

Thomas Gainsborough's statue in Sudbury
(By kind permission of Gainsborough's House Society)

paint in Sudbury. One of his first works in Ipswich was painting Mrs Cobbold and her daughter, (the family would become associated with the notorious Margaret Catchpole, who was twice reprieved from hanging).

Many of Gainsborough's paintings, during this period of time, are to be found in Gainsborough's House, in the street which is now named after him, in Sudbury. It is well worth a visit and highly recommended.

In the late 1750s Gainsborough moved to Bath where he wanted to take his career along a more individual style. This he achieved and, in 1768, became a founder member of the Royal Academy. Six years later he moved to London and, very quickly, (and not many people know this), he became established as unofficial painter to the royal family. (Could have done the master's drawing room a different colour, though!)

Gainsborough died at the age of 61, at the pinnacle of his fame and notoriety. He left a lasting legacy for all to enjoy, thanks to the work of many of his supporters. In the early 1900s, many of his paintings were starting to leave the country and being bought by overseas galleries and tycoons. We have perhaps lost forever his most celebrated work, *Blue Boy*, to America. But the tide has turned and, in 1913, a national monument was unveiled on Market Hill, in Sudbury, and, of course, Gainsborough's House was opened to the public in 1961. So he will live on – where he was born – in Sudbury.

John Constable

One cannot mention one without the other, and John Constable, along with Thomas Gainsborough, (must be *suffen* in the Suffolk air), are looked upon as two of the most prominent artists that England has ever seen!

Constable was born in East Bergholt in 1776, and at an early age *shew* a desire for drawing. Although he went to a private boarding school in Lavenham, where all the boys were flogged mercilessly, and later to Dedham Grammar School, it was not the art masters who influenced his creative artistic flair. No! It was back in East Bergholt, where John would spend hours with a neighbouring plumber and glazier, by the name of John Dunthone, who was a local landscape artist. What an influence this practically unknown artist must have had on John. It was Constable *hisself*, some years later, who is reputed to have said, 'Scenes of my boyhood, made me a painter'. It goes to show, just how much input Dunthone must have had for Constable to make that statement – Enormous!

In 1795 Constable went to London to see if he could be a successful painter.

(Suffolk Record Office, Ipswich – ref K681/2/80/24)

He met up with John Thomas Smith, who was a draughtsman, engraver and local antiquarian, and was known as 'Antiquity Smith', (a vast improvement on John Thomas Smith!).

Constable tried to start his artistic career as an etcher, but not too successfully, and he returned to work for his father. His itching for etching had not dwindled, and he turned his hand once again to the pencil. In 1799, he was accepted into the Royal Academy and, two years later, set up a studio at 50 Rathbone Place, London. He started to exhibit his work, which included a drawing in 1806 called, *HMS Victory in The Battle of Trafalgar between two French Ships of the Line* – Didn't they have unnecessarily long titles? He had been inspired by hearing the account from a Suffolk sailor, who had served alongside Lord Nelson on the *Victory*.

From 1810 onwards, Constable suffered from bad health and once again returned to his beloved East Bergholt, where he slowly recovered. In 1816 and, after a six-year courtship, (remember, he was a Suffolk lad!), he finally got wed to Maria Bicknell. They had seven children, (not much wrong with his health now!), and from the 1820s onwards became quite prolific in his output of painting landscapes. The list is extensive and includes, in 1821, the painting of *The Haywain* which, some of you might know, appeared on the front cover of my book *Sloightly on th' Huh!*.

Sadly for John, his wife died in 1828, and thereafter he lived the rest of his life suffering from deep depression. He was never the same again, but what a lasting effect he's had on the artistic world. Not only that, he has made one part of Suffolk, in and around East Bergholt, world famous, just by painting.

CHAPTER 5

Suffolk Surnames

More and more people today are researching their family trees. They are also trying to find out what their surnames mean. And as such, 'Haylock's Half Hour for Forty Minutes' every Thursday, has proved to be a hit on BBC Radio Suffolk's Lesley Dolphin's show, *All About Suffolk*. Each week, we're gradually working through the alphabet with Suffolk surnames, and the listeners' response is just fantastic. Thank you kindly.

Why do we have Suffolk surnames like **Aldous**, **Baalham**, **Cocksedge**, **Eastaugh**, **Feveyear** and **Finbow**? And others, like **Garnham**, **Gooderham**, **Hagwood** and **Howgegow**? What makes these surnames, and many, many more, peculiarly Suffolk?

But first ...
Why We Have Surnames

Before the Conquest, the English, with their Anglo-Saxon/Viking mix, did not have surnames. They gave each other descriptive personal names, and it was all about recognising people and distinguishing *theirselves* from one another. *Howsumever*, the ruling chieftains, or well-to-do families may have had a name that was sometimes haphazardly handed down.

After the Conquest in 1066, William the Conqueror and his administrators introduced the concept of having surnames, to be passed on down the family line. This was very foreign to the English, but gradually the idea caught on, and by the mid 1400s (I did say gradually – this is Suffolk after all!), it was considered vulgar not to have a surname.

But it was still common, up to this time, for English couples to have several children all with different surnames. (What a scandal that would cause today – be the talk of the village!). It was still all about distinguishing one another from each other. For example, an English couple could have three children: Ethelred **Edison** (Edward's son), Hilda **Blunt** (Anglo-Saxon for 'blonde') and Matilda **Crack** (bright shiny black hair).

Also, one person could have several surnames during their life span, eg. Alfred the **Fairchild** grows up to become a carpenter, and could then be called Alfred **Carpenter,** who, in turn, moves away from his village of Debenham, and then could be called Alfred de **Debenham**. All very confusing to us but not to the English at the time.

Then they started to impose dastardly, fiendish taxes like the poll tax, and it became essential for surnames to be passed down the family line. Now we did have confusion! And there was no 'Confused.com' in *them* days!

Bill Baker was so-called, because he was the village baker.
He had a grown-up son, who was also called Bill, after his father.
This Bill was the village butcher and, accordingly, had been called Bill Butcher.
He too had a son called Bill who became a local bowman and went by the name of Bill Bowman.
So we now have Bill Baker the baker and his son,
Bill Butcher, the butcher, and his son, Bill Bowman, the bowman.

All very logical because surnames still meant a way of identifying people. But that was all about to change. It gets wusser!

And we then got ... are you ready for this? ...

Bill Baker the baker has a son called Bill Baker,
who still is the butcher but not Bill Butcher and is now Bill Baker,
the same name as Bill Baker the baker.
Now ... Bill Baker the butcher, and not the baker, has a son called Bill Baker,
who is still the bowman but not Bill Bowman and is now Bill Baker,
the same name as Bill Baker the butcher and Bill Baker the baker

So, we now have ...

Bill Baker, who's the bowman, but not the butcher nor the baker,
the son of Bill Baker, who's the butcher, but not the baker nor the bowman,

*who's the son of Bill Baker, who's not the butcher nor the bowman,
but who is the baker ... Bill Baker,
the same name as Bill Baker and Bill Baker who aren't bakers.
But, Bill Baker is still the baker!*

Confused.com?!!!!

Only Four Types of Surname

Place Names – These ranged from very local names like William who lives down the **Lane**, or in the **Wood** (**Atwood, Attewood** or **Underwood**), or lives in the **Hills** or works in the **Field** etc, etc. Moving away from a village or town to live somewhere else could end up, Richard from Hadleigh (**Hadley**), or Robert from Finborough (**Finbow**), and Alfred from Debenham (**Debnam**). The names were often spelled as they were said. The surname **Suffolk** originated in Essex. Sounds rather strange I know, but whilst an *owd Suffolker* lived in Suffolk he was no different to anyone else, because they all lived in Suffolk, and it wouldn't distinguish him from anyone else. But as soon as he moved to Essex, he was then known as Richard **Suffolk**, because he was different from the others. – Very different in this case!

Trades – These are fairly self explanatory: Will the **Butcher**, Alfred the **Fletcher**, etc, etc and these tend to be fairly widespread nationally, eg **Smith**. But there are some Suffolk based trade names, eg **Ashman, Blok** and **Botman,** as you will see later, on the Surname list.

Nicknames – Lots of names derive from nicknames, which then became personal names, and then surnames at a later date. There are far too many to mention, but a few examples include **Fairchild, Armstrong, Goodbody** and **Faires** (good old Suffolk name, that one!). All the colours are nicknames due to the colour of the clothes they wore or the colour of their hair or the colour of their complexion: **Black, White, Greene, Red**, etc, and **Redhead.** It could be that someone behaved like a **King**, or behaved like a **Monk**, a **Priest** or an **Abbott**. The last three wouldn't have had any offspring to pass the name down to, because they were celibate, (well, supposed to be), and therefore they were also nicknames.

Anglo-Saxons had many legends about the elf, who was considered noble

The Local Baker delivering in Crowfield
(Coddenham History Club)

and bold, tall and blond, virile and beautiful, and excelled in every aspect of life; not the tiny little hobgoblin fellow we think of today. There were also the legends relating to the wolf who was strong and protective, powerful and ferocious, and was the leader of the pack. These elf and wolf legends gave rise to many nicknames and they still survive today through surnames, especially in Suffolk surnames, as you will see also from the Surname list.

Sons of, Family of – This section takes on many more surname endings than just **son**, and some are quite surprising. One, in particular, needs a careful explanation.

Son This tiny little word was brought over by the Vikings in the 8th and 9th century onwards (eg Leif **Ericsson**, Magnus **Magnusson**, Sven Goran **Ericsson**, **Robson**, **Wilson**, etc, etc). This next fact is astounding. Even today, geographical distribution of surnames ending in **son** accurately reflect the extent of the Viking invasions over a thousand years ago. Some 50% of

Yorkshire surnames end in **son**, 45% of the surnames from the North-East of England, with only 10% in Suffolk and just 1% in Cornwall.

Kin – meaning 'family of', as in **Wilkins**, **Atkins**, etc, etc, sometimes extended later to **Wilkinson** and **Atkinson**.

Ling or **Ing** – This is pure Anglo-Saxon and means the 'young of' or 'follower of', as in the words **duckling**, **gosling**, **fledgling**, **sibling** and **following**. This also reflects in surnames like **Hubling** and **Manning**.

Cock – This is where I have to be careful. The Anglo-Saxon word for 'tap' is 'cock', as in stopcock and ballcock. It was very important for Anglo-Saxons to have male heirs, and so when babies were born, the first thing they looked for was the little 'tap', to see if it was a boy. 'Cock' was a normal everyday word in Anglo-Saxon times, and it became a pet word for 'son', as in **Peacock**, (Peter's son), **Adcock** (Adam's son), **Willcox** (Will's son), etc, etc. Londoners still use it today when they say, 'Watcha cock!' and even interpret it for us when they say, 'Hello son'. Both mean the same. It was not until the 1700s when 'cock' became the vulgar word it is today. Surnames ending in **cock**, are mainly found in East Anglia, the Midlands and southern England – not up North! There – that wasn't too hard, was it?!

Howsumever, **Alecock, Glasscock** and **Woodcock** could refer to trade names rather than 'sons of'.

Ett, Ott – This is a Norman suffix and means 'little' as in cigar and cigarette (little cigar). It's just the same in surnames and is the Norman way of denoting a son or daughter. **Bennett** (little Ben, instead of Benson), **Willmott,** (little William, instead of Wilson), **Philpott,** (little Philip, instead of Philipson), Marriot, (little Mary, instead of Mary's daughter), etc, etc.

What Makes It a Suffolk Surname?

Surnames first appear in the Domesday Book in 1086, and obviously there is a fair collection of Norman names. But some of the forward-thinking English (the best part of a fair few from Suffolk), especially the more renowned, had grasped the idea and started to use surnames, and were also recorded in this great survey. As a matter of interest, there were two Domesday Books, the Great and the Little. The latter was for Suffolk, Essex and Norfolk only, as that was the most densely populated area of the country. It needed more scribes to complete it and ended up being more detailed than the Great Domesday Book itself. Gradually, when the English went to court, or paid their taxes, or had land disputes, or were part of the church, or were granted a royal charter, or purchased some land, etc, etc, their surnames would get recorded for the first time in the various records of the day. These were usually in the form of rolls of parchment, as it was too expensive to keep making books.

Surnames were being recorded in the Suffolk Subsidy Rolls (tax records), Suffolk Assize Rolls (court records, usually financial), Suffolk Curia Regis Rolls (King's Court records), Suffolk Pipe Rolls (more general), Suffolk Feet of Fines (land disputes), Suffolk Hundred Rolls (detailed survey of the various Hundreds), and other similar documents.

During this period, many of the Anglo-Saxon personal names and nicknames were also being turned into surnames for the first time. Some of these recorded surnames were peculiar to Suffolk and have remained so.

Mr T.G. Alecock
(The Windmill House Collection)

Mrs R.J. Alecock
(The Windmill House Collection)

Outside the Corset Factory
(The Jerv Jordan Collection)

Therefore I have classed them as Suffolk surnames. Through time, Suffolk has also evolved its own variations of more common surnames, peculiar only to Suffolk. I've included those too.

A few surnames seem to have started in a number of places, including Suffolk, but have fizzled out elsewhere quite early on and have become virtually extinct – except in Suffolk. I've included those few, too.

And last but not least, by looking at the various surname distribution records, there are still surnames appearing in Suffolk, and nowhere else. I've included those as well.

With so many surnames to go through, the list has been limited to the first part of the alphabet: A to L, and the remainder will be part of the next book.

SUFFOLK SURNAMES A – L

Albrey Anglo-Saxon for Elf or Noble king.
Alby Comes from 'Albin' which is Norman -French for 'white'.
Aldous An Anglo-Saxon female name.
Aldredge/Aldrich Anglo-Saxon for Elf or Noble ruler.
Alecock Anglo-Saxon for either **son of Al** or a trade, **ale cock** (beer tap) – taps up Anglo-Saxon beer barrels. I prefer the latter meaning!
Alfleet Anglo-Saxon for Elf or Noble beauty (must have been a cracker).
Allvey Anglo-Saxon for Elf or Noble warrior.
Allward Anglo-Saxon for Elf or Noble guard.
Amass Norman French for friend, **amis**.
Angier/Ainger Norman French – someone from Angers, France.

Mr 'Jack' Aldrich (1879–1975). (courtesy of Jo Miles)

Anness Norman French for Agnes.

Arbon Danish name, Arn Bjorn.

Artist/Arters Norman French – someone from Artois, France.

Ashman Anglo-Saxon nickname for a sailor or pirate.

Baalam/Baalham/Balaam From Baylham, Suffolk.

Bardwell From Bardwell, Suffolk.

Baskett A basket maker.

Battisford From Battisford, Suffolk .

Bedingfield From Bedingfield, Suffolk .

Block /Blok A blocker. One who uses a block, eg a shoemaker or bookmaker.

Bloomfield/ Blomfield/ Blomefield Norman French for someone from Blonville sur Mer, France.

Blowers Anglo-Saxon name for a hornblower.

Boggis Anglo-Saxon nickname for someone who blusters and brags.

Bossom from Bosome meaning Boatswain, and for hundreds of years, only recorded in Beccles, Suffolk.

Botwright Anglo-Saxon for maker of boats.

Brewington Records show, from the lost village of Brewington in Suffolk.

Brightwell From Brightwell, Suffolk.

Brummer Anglo-Saxon for brown frame (swarthy, or colour of hair or clothes).

Brundish From Brundish, Suffolk.

Ernest Walter Baalham.
(courtesy of Heather Welch, née Baalham)

Brunwin Anglo-Saxon for brown friend (swarthy, or colour of hair or clothes).

Buckledee First recorded in 1761 in Whatfield – meaning not yet found but all Buckledees can be traced back to Whatfield 1761.

Buckles Buckle-maker.

Bugg/Buggs Anglo-Saxon nickname for scarecrow or hobgoblin.

Bullett Norman French nickname meaning round and little.

Bullard Anglo-Saxon trade name for bull yard or bull guard.

Burward Anglo-Saxon name for a guard at a fort – burgh ward.

Buttrum/Bartrum Anglo-Saxon nickname for bright raven – black shiny hair.

Byham/Byam Someone who lives just outside the village – by ham.

Cable Anglo-Saxon meaning 'famous and bold', or Anglo-French meaning 'cable for a ropemaker', or Middle English 'cabal', meaning a horse or horseman.

Cady Anglo-Saxon nickname for a stout person.

Canham First recorded as *Cauenham* – someone from Cavenham, Suffolk.

Catchpole Anglo-Saxon catcher of poultry from debtors, later, a tax collector.

Cattermole Meaning unknown, but from Flemish or Dutch weavers.

Chason/Chasten Dweller by the chestnut tree.

Chattin Anglo-Saxon nickname 'Catting' pronounced 'chatting', meaning cat- like, agile and quick, or lucky, (nine lives). It doesn't mean someone who talks a lot!

Chenery/Chinnery Norman French for someone from Chenevray, France.

Cobbold Anglo-Saxon for famous and bold.

Cockrill Norman French for seller of poultry. Note: 'cockerel' for male chicken didn't come into use until the mid 1400s. Therefore **Cockrill** doesn't refer to a male chicken.

Cocksedge Anglo-Saxon for dweller by the edge of the hill.

Cone Norman French for dweller by corner where roads meet.

Copping Anglo-Saxon for dweller on the top of a hill.

Copen Suffolk way of pronouncing '**Copping**' – as above.

Cordle Norman French for cord or rope maker.

Cotwin Anglo-Saxon friend who provides shelter .

Crack Anglo-Saxon nickname for one with black, shiny hair.

Cracknell An Anglo-Saxon named **Crack**, living somewhere secluded.

James Catchpole 1818–1902. Photo c1890.
Note: Father was James Catchpool, born 1796 in Barnham.
(courtesy of Neil, Kim and Alice Catchpole)

Crannis Anglo-Saxon nickname for long-legged, like a **crane** (crannish).

Crowford Someone who lives by a 'crow ford' – a ford by a tributary or where a river splits in two – resembling a crow's foot.

Crofford Suffolk pronunciation of **Crowford** as above.

Crowfoot Anglo-Saxon for buttercup – possibly very yellow hair – or wore a buttercup in a hat – or lived by a buttercup meadow

Curdy Norman French for rope or cord maker

Dade Anglo-Saxon for famous deed or exploit

Dallinger From Dallinghoo, Suffolk .

Dansie d'Anesi – Norman French – someone from Anisy, in Normandy.

Debenham/Debnam From Debenham, Suffolk

Deck Anglo-Saxon 'dic' – dweller by the ditch or dyke.

Denington/ Dennington From Dennington, Suffolk.

Drawsword Anglo-Saxon, probably for a knight or similar.

Duet Pet form of Juliana, Juet or Jouet, hence pronunciation 'duet'.

Dunnage From Dunwich, pronounced 'dunnage'

Durrant Old French for obstinate

Eagle Like the bird – a nickname.

Eary Dweller in a shieling – a mobile home, eg a shepherd's hut.

Eastaugh/Easto Anglo-Saxon for dweller by the east field or ridge.

Eckhart Anglo-Saxon for edge hard, perhaps a strong swordsman.

Elman Anglo-Saxon for seller of oil, vegetable oil, etc – not diesel oil!

Elwood Anglo-Saxon for Elf or Noble guard – the same as **Allward**.

Emery Norm French for hard worker.

Everett/Everitt Anglo-Saxon nickname for 'boar hard' – a tough fighter.

Everson Son of Evot, which in itself means daughter of Eve or Eva.

Eye Anglo-Saxon for dweller on dry land surrounded by marsh or water.

Faires/ Faiers/Fayres Anglo-Saxon for fair and beautiful.

Farrants Norman French for iron grey, perhaps colour of hair or clothes.

Farthing Anglo-Saxon *foerding* for a fourth part; dweller at a home or a farmstead in four parts (eg split between four sons).

Feveyear/ Feaviour Middle English for someone born in February.

Finbow From Finborough, Suffolk.

Fisk Viking pronunciation of fish /a fisherman.

Flatman Man who lives on flat land.

Flatt Danish for dweller on flat level ground.

Flory Norman French for someone from Fleury, France. Other variations of

Nana Ellen Farthing, with Grandson Ronnie.
(courtesy of Vivienne Leeder, née Farthing)

The Feveyear Family 1936
(courtesy of Doug Feveyear, Hadleigh.)

spelling are more widespread, but **Flory** is Suffolk.

Foller Old English trade name – a fuller of raw cloth, (preparing before use).

Footer Old Norse nickname for someone with big feet.

Foulger Anglo-Saxon for soldier.

Freston From Freston, Suffolk.

Gaffer/ Gayfer Norman French for maker of iron hooks – a gaff is an iron hook.

Gallington Anglo-Saxon for someone living on land owned by a relative or friend.

Game/Gayman Anglo-Saxon for a dealer in game.

Gandey Anglo-Saxon for someone who works for a dealer in game.

Gant Three options: Middle English for tall slender and angular; Norman French *gaunt* for glove maker/seller, hence gauntlet;

(courtesy of Dave Feaviour & Margaret Thompson)

Peasenhall Quoits Championship.
Frank Garnham (front, left) was also Suffolk County Singles
Quoits Champion 1938. (courtesy of Janice Feller)

– from Ghent Flemish weavers. It would appear that the Suffolk **Gants** are weavers from Ghent.

Garneys Norman French for moustache.

Garnham Norman French for wearing a moustache.

Garrod/Garro Norman French for 'Brave Spear' - a warrior.

Garwood Anglo-Saxon for yard guard. A yard was roughly 30 acres worked by peasants; part of the manorial feudal system.

Gaselee/ Gazelee/Gazeley From Gazeley, Suffolk.

Gassman/Gastman A man owing allegiance to a feudal lord called Gass (or similar).

Gathercole A nickname for an old man who had gathered cold. It was said that when old, a man's blood would dry and wax and go cold.

Gildersleeve(s) Anglo-Saxon for a man with a golden sleeve.

Gipson/Gypson Saxon pronunciation of Yippsing, descendants of Yipps. **Yipps** was the first Angle invader to build the first Angle settlement known as **Yippswiche**, later to be known as Ipswich. Therefore, someone called **Gipson** could be descended from the first Angle invader. Wow!

Girling Corruption of Norman French *Coeur de lion*, which became Girdelion, then Girdling, and eventually Girling.

Gislam From Gisleham, Suffolk.

Gladwell Dweller by a stream in a glade.

Gleeman/Glewman Anglo-Saxon gleoman – a minstrel.

Gobbett Anglo-Saxon nickname 'go better'.

Godbold Anglo-Saxon nickname for gold bold.

Goldbard/Goldbart Anglo-Saxon nickname for golden beard.

Goldspink Anglo-Saxon for goldfinch.

Golson Anglo-Saxon nickname for gold stone.

Gooderham Viking nickname for battle snake, which is also the name of the first Danish ruler of East Anglia. Therefore, someone called Gooderham could be descended from ancient Viking royal stock.

Gort Local pronunciation of Norman French *court* – resident or employee at large house, manor house or castle.

Goymer Anglo-Saxon for battle famous.

Gravlin Norman French for someone from Gravelines, Normandy.

Greader/ Greeder Middle English for town crier.

Greengrass/Greengres(s) Viking for dweller by a green, grassy place.

Greenleaf Anglo-Saxon nickname for a green leaf.

Sniper Jack Garrod during the Great War 1914–18. (courtesy of Rex Garrod)

Griggs Son of Gregory.
Grimsey An area of dry land, surrounded by water or marshlands, belonging to someone named Grimes.
Grimwood Anglo-Saxon nickname for a helmet guard.
Haggin Dweller on farm-holding.
Hagwood Anglo-Saxon for someone who maintained and guarded hedges.
Haken Viking for noble class.
Haker Anglo-Saxon for one who hacks, (probably a wood cutter) or a maker of hacks, (agricultural tools such as mattocks and hoes).
Halesworth From Halesworth, Suffolk.
Hammitt The son of someone who lives on low lying land by a stream.
Hardgrove Dweller by a grove where the ground is hard or hard to work.
Hayhoe Angle pronunciation for dweller by the high ridge.
Howgegow Saxon pronunciation of Hayhoe – as above
Haylock Son of an Angle Chieftain Hagul (pronounced *Hay'l*)
Hibble Pet form of 'Isabel'.
Hillen Tihel de Helean, 'The Breton', came over with William the Conqueror and, as such, was granted land in Suffolk. **Hillen** is a direct descendant of Tihel de Helean.

Helm't guaard?
Oi should a bin a
Grimwood shoon't
Oi?

Harry Grimwood (top left) in Egypt during the Second World War.
(courtesy of the Grimwood Family, Boxford.)

Holdbow Anglo-Saxon nickname for gracious and bright.
Hollen Anglo-Saxon for dweller by the holm-oak or holly oak.
Hollox Dweller in the small hollow.
Hubling Son of Hubb, (Hubb is short for 'Hubert').
Hufflet Son of Hugh.
Hulver Viking for holly tree, dweller by a holly tree.
Hurren/Hurron Norman French for shaggy haired. Not to be confused with 'heron'. Heron came from the Anglo-Saxon word *harensaw*.
Husting Viking for officer of a law-court.
Ingate Someone from Ingate, Suffolk.
Jaye Like the bird – and a nickname for a chatterer.

William Arthur Haylock, 1889–1979. (The Windmill Collection)

Jowers Norman French for a journeyman.

Kant Variation of Cant – Old French for singing – a minstrel.

Keeble Anglo-Saxon for a maker or seller of cudgels.

Kentell/ Kentwell Someone from Kentwell, Suffolk.

Kenrich/Kerridge Anglo-Saxon for a family ruler.

Kersey From Kersey, Suffolk.

Kindred Local vicar of Carlton cum Kelsale found a baby left on his doorstep. Not knowing the name of the baby, he said that it was his 'kindred' and therefore gave the baby that surname.

Knappett Dweller on top of a small hillock.

Laflin Viking name meaning 'from the land of fjords'.

Larner /Lerner Directly descended from Edmund de Lauueney, who came from Larner's Wood in Little Saxham, Suffolk.

Last Anglo-Saxon for a shoemaker's wooden foot mould; therefore, a maker of lasts or a shoemaker.

Leathers Dealer in leather.

Leeks Seller of leeks.

Leist Old German for wood – a woodcutter or someone who works in wood.

Leiston From Leiston, Suffolk.

Level Anglo-Saxon nickname for a beloved ruler.

Ling Viking for heather – someone who lives near the heather.

Litwin Anglo-Saxon for light or bright friend.

Longliff Anglo-Saxon nickname meaning long life.

Should you want a more detailed explanation on these good *owd* Suffolk names, then please log on to my website, **www.charliehaylock.com** and visit the Suffolk Surnames page. It will give details of the date the surname was first recorded, how it was originally spelled, a fuller meaning, and other variations.

I hope you find what you are looking for.

(courtesy of Tim and Sarah Kindred)

CHAPTER 6

The Suffolk Abacus

My grandfather *shew* me this enthralling clever Suffolk invention when I was a lad. He'd been taught it at Stanstead school, near Long Melford, when he was a *booy*. He was told it was the Suffolk abacus, and I have found no evidence to dispute it.

Grandfather was born in 1889. Times in Suffolk were hard and when he was at school, at the turn of the last century, he knew he'd be having a lot of time off. Not bunking off and not playing truant neither. Oh, no!

If there was gleaning for wheat to do, after the harvest, then the whole family went. It was essential to collect as much corn as you could. They were gathering the family year's supply. This would later be thrashed, and then ground down into flour, which was then used to bake their bread throughout the year! Everyone went *tater* picking or fruit picking, including the *young 'ns*. It was essential; they had to pull their weight, else they would starve.

How did the schools deal with this absenteeism? They adapted their teaching methods and streamlined it in order to teach as much as they could in the time they had. This obviously applied to arithmetic as well, and an ingenious Suffolk abacus evolved.

The young school children were taught their 2, 3, 4, 5 and 10 times tables thoroughly. Once they had grasped this, then the rest was simple, easy and quick. By using their hands and fingers, the school children were able to work out their 6, 7, 8 and 9 times tables, easily – in a flash! I have drawn diagrams to explain this incredible simple system.

The children held out their hands with their palms facing them, with fingers splayed out. The hands would be pointing towards one another but not touching. The fingers on each hand were then given numbers. The little fingers were both 6 and the next finger would be 7. Both the middle fingers would be 8 and the index fingers 9.

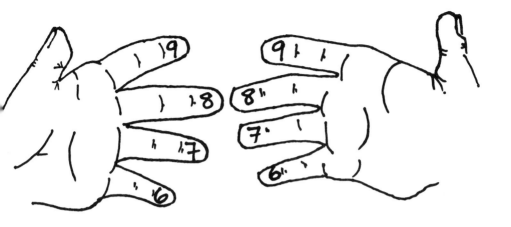

Now the fun begins and we can do our multiplication.

8 multiplied by 8

Point the two 8 fingers, (the middle fingers), towards one another and touch.

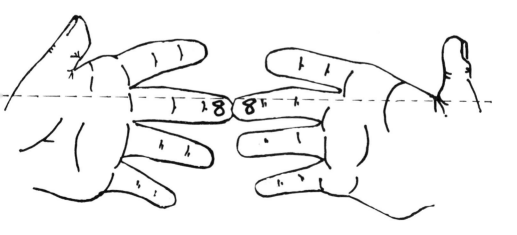

You then count the number of fingers that are touching and below and multiply by 10. In this case, that's 6 fingers and multiply by 10, which equals 60.

Then above the touching fingers you have two digits, (a finger and a thumb) on one hand and the same on the other. Multiply the two together, 2 x 2 which equals 4 and add on to the 60. The answer – 64.

9 multiplied by 6

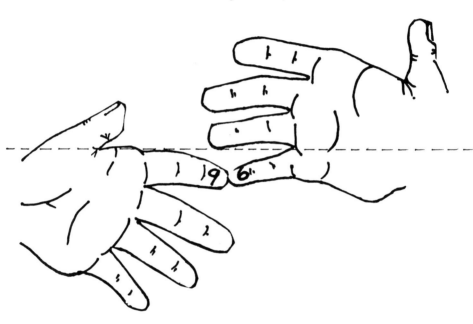

Point the 9 finger, (the index finger), towards the 6 finger, (little finger), and touch.

You then count the number of fingers that are touching and below and multiply by 10. In this case, that's 5 fingers and multiply by 10, which equals 50.

Then above the touching fingers you have four digits on one hand and one on the other. Multiply the two together, 4 x 1 which equals 4 and add on to the 50. The answer – 54.

It works whatever multiplication you want. Try it and see. You'll be amazed!

CHAPTER 7

Suffolk Squit

What is Suffolk squit?

Thas loike Norf'lk nonsense, but jest a bit ...

What is Suffolk squit?

It tends to be situational and a final one-liner comment on that situation, completely in the opposite direction to which people are thinking. Some people think it's the dead pan face, throwaway, one-liner. There's nothing throw away about it. Generally, that one-liner is so full of meaning that you could write a book about it. The cartoon example of the townie taking a short cut sums it up completely, as does the tale about the four-minute warning. But then again, Suffolk squit can be absolute nonsense, almost 'Goonish'.

The constant straight face makes it very difficult, nigh on impossible, for strangers to distinguish between the poignant one-liner and the nonsense. Only Suffolk people instinctively can do that and, of course, Norfolk! I must readily admit that, and very pleased to do so. We wouldn't have Suffolk Norfolk banter otherwise! And that certainly wouldn't do!

Howsumever, I had a few *mardles* with some good *owd* friends of mine, Rex Garrod, the eccentric creative engineer associated with Doctor Who's K9, Neil Catchpole, the 'Warbling Woodman' and Jerv Jordan, the Suffolk Show commentator on vintage tractors. They all have *suffen* in common – squit! I asked them the question, 'What is Suffolk squit?' Well we couldn't stop laughing as we heard each other's stories. Some of these are *writ* down here as tales, others converted into cartoons and some are captions on archive photos. Hopefully, this is Suffolk squit at its best.

The Four-Minute Warning

It was an evening in the local pub, not long after there had been discussions in Parliament about nuclear energy and nuclear weapons. The pub was not too far from Sizewell and the nuclear power station. The pub was fairly full with people from other parts and not many locals at all, if any, except the *owd* boy sat in the corner all on his own, minding his own business, just slowly drinking his pint, but listening intently. Truly, Suffolk.

Obviously it wasn't very long afore the discussions were of a nuclear nature and were both local and topical, and very quickly got on to nuclear warfare. Eventually the question was asked, 'What would you do if there was a four-minute warning?'

Everyone started to divulge their four-minute escapades and what they would be getting up to, and some were quite explicit.

Then, suddenly, one of the gathered throng asked the *owd* boy in the corner what would he do if there was a four-minute warning. Everyone waited for his reply. He put his pint down, looked at everyone and said, very thoughtfully and slowly,

'Oi'd tayke a good foive minnuts at least, think'n abowt ut.'

Everyone laughed, but not for the right reason. They didn't understand. And then they started to take the mickey,

'Silly old fool!' 'Be too bloody late – you'll be dead and gone before you've decided what to do!'

'Arrr,' he said, 'at least Oi'll goo with happy thoughts.'

They all looked puzzled and asked what he had meant.

'Whoilst yew duzzy buggers are tear arrs'n abowt, troying ter dew whot yew say yew would dew, but never dew dew, in tootal panic,' he said, with just a hint of a glint in his eye, but still dead pan, 'Oi'll be sitt'n there, awl noice and calm, with moy hid full of awl them lovely things Oi'd be dew'n, whoilst yew're rush'n arownd still troy'n ter dew 'em, but not dew'n 'em.'

They didn't take the mickey any more and, in fact, he had quite a few pints bought him that night.

The Owd Suffolk Farmer and the Young Barmaid

The local farmer, who went by the nickname of Troff was 65 years of age, and was a confirmed bachelor; had never had a girlfriend in his life. Although there were some talk and whispers way back in the seventies but we don't mention that. He had great 'job satisfaction' from his farming, and had won many a trophy at the Suffolk Show for his livestock, especially his Suffolk Red Poll and his Suffolk sheep. He also kept Suffolk Punches and used them principally as working horses, although he had many a rosette for 'Best of Breed'. He also took great pride on the arable side of things, and also won many a trophy for his spring barley and winter wheat at the local Farmers Association's presentation night.

He was old-fashioned and set in his ways, and didn't want life cluttered up with taking on a wife. That would seriously upset his routine far beyond any reasonable level of acceptance.

He enjoyed his daily visit to the local pub of an evening, and supped a *couple a three* pints of Suffolk brewed ale out of his pewter mug, (another trophy for 'Best of' *suffen* or other). He didn't say much, especially not to *furreners.* He only really spoke to 'real' locals now and again during the course of the evening, very profoundly, with an underlying hint of Suffolk humour when he did. He was certainly not a conversationalist.

Then it happened. His life suddenly changed. His local pub went and employed a new barmaid called Elspeth. He was love-struck immediately he first clapped eyes on her. *Howsumever,* the one big problem here was, although she was single and available, she was a young *gal* in her early twenties. Troff was in his mid sixties, but a changed man.

He actually started wearing smart casual clothes when he went up the pub, and not his usual working clobber. He became very talkative, especially across the bar, and *suffen* must have happened between 'em. Suddenly, there was a whirlwind romance. It was the talk of the village. You know how it is – 'Owd enough to be her father' – 'On't last' – 'Dutty owd bugger' – 'What does she see in he?' – 'Thinks he'll win more trophies with her, 'at's whoy' – and so it went on.

And then, and then, 'The Day' was announced! They were to be wed after this two-month relationship – the very next week! No engagement, straight into it.

Well, 'The Day' came and went, and Troff and Elspeth went away for a honeymoon weekend in Wells-next-the-Sea in Norfolk. They couldn't go for longer than a weekend in Norfolk (and that's NOT a ding at Norfolk this time, although it could be). He just couldn't leave his farm for too long.

Elspeth immediately did the old-fashioned thing and gave up being a barmaid, to become a farmer's wife. It wasn't till about a week later, that Troff visited the local for his usual pint or two. He walked in through the door and, immediately, there was silence.

Then suddenly, 'Even'n Troff'.

'Even'n t'gether', was Troff's reply.

Locals were now winking at one another, nudging and whispering.

Troff ordered his pint, and stood in his usual corner, leant on the bar, all by *hisself*, just smiling.

Eventually it had to happen. Everyone was dying to know and a group sidled over to Troff, and quietly asked, 'What's ut loike then, being married to a young gal loike 'at?'

'Yer know', says Troff, shrugging his shoulders.

They asked again and got the same response. So they decided to buy him a few beers. And when they thought the time was right, they asked him again.

'Jest a few problems at fust ..... nuthen Oi couldn't handle though,' he said.

'What dew yew mean?' they asked.

'Yer know', says Troff, shrugging his shoulders.

So they decided to buy him a few more beers. And when they thought the time was right, they asked him again.

'Jest a few problems at fust ..... nuthen Oi couldn't handle though,' he said, 'Oi couldn't keep moy hands off her.'

'Call that a problem!?' they all cried.

'Yes, 'at wuz a problem, nuthen Oi couldn't handle though,' he said.

'What did yew dew!?' they all shouted.

'Oi sacked all moy hands,' he said calmly. He finished his pint and bid them all, 'Good noight t'gether,' as he made for the door. As he was just about to leave, he turned and said, 'Thanks for all the drinks t'gether.' They all then knew that they'd all been had!

The Empty Grave in the Churchyard

This is a story told by a typical *owd* Suffolker, 'Doody' Corncroft. He was nicknamed Doody, as that's the *owd* Suffolk dialect word for 'little', and Doody wasn't very tall – about 5 ft 4 ins in his boots.

He explained how there had been a night of revelry up the local. It was a pub well ahead of its time, running flexi hours well afore the Government introduced the new licensing laws. The local football team had just won the Suffolk Cup Final at Portman Road, which was the home of Ipswich Town, a Premiership League ground, (that's then, not now – much to the enjoyment of Norwich City fans).

Everyone was *dint* of wine and tipsy, including Doody. It was time to go home and off Doody set. It was a dark *owd* night, and Doody felt a storm a-coming on so he decided to take a short cut through the churchyard. Unbeknown to Doody, the grave digger, earlier that day, had prepared a grave

Dealer, c.1890, Barrow (Suffolk Record Office, Ipswich – ref K681/1/27/3)

for a funeral the next day. He'd left the job in a hurry and failed to cover up the grave.

You have guessed the inevitable. Doody staggered across the churchyard and fell into the waiting hole, with a *hellava* thud. He got up, dusted *hisself* down, said a *couple a three* choice words, and proceeded to try and get out of the grave. It could have been his height, it could have been the drink, it could have been a mixture of both, but the more Doody tried to climb out the grave, the more he couldn't.

He decided to sit down, huddled up, in the corner and ponder his predicament, and try to hit on a solution to the problem. Some twenty minutes later, Doody had a bit of a shock. *Owd* 'Thatch' Whymonger, so-called because of his mop of blond hair, had gone and done the self same thing.

Doody went on to explain, 'Owd Thatch hit the grou'nd with a thud. He stood up with his back ter me and looked uppards. Reckon he wuz troy'n to figger a way owt. Well, Oi tapped 'm on the shoulder gently and quietly say, 'Yew on't get owt a heeyer booy'...... Well, he did .... and bluddy quick tew.'

(Drawings by Gale – characters by Barrie Appleby)

(Coddenham History Club)

(Suffolk Record Office, Ipswich – ref K681/1/27/4)

CHAPTER 8

Suffolk Landmarks

I always enjoy this section. We have so much to celebrate in Suffolk!

I like to pick out some of the not so obvious, as well as the traditional ones. I'd also like to have perhaps an irreverent look at some, but all are true Suffolk landmarks for one reason or another.

The Hollesley Bay Colony Stud

The first one I have selected is the Hollesley Bay Colony Stud, home of the Suffolk Punch Trust. I visited there recently and was well impressed. It is fair

Suffolks Ploughing
Photograph kindly donated by Kit Houghton to
The Suffolk Punch Trust

(By kind permission of The Suffolk Punch Trust)

to say, that if it had not been for the Suffolk Punch Trust, then the world famous Suffolk working horse could well be extinct, and gone forever. This cannot happen! It is still a rare breed so a lot more work is still needed.

The Trust at Hollesley is on the original site of Sink Farm, which was part of the Red House Estate and, according to the records, Suffolk Punches were on the farm in 1759, and have been there ever since. The site has taken on many guises through the years, and in 2006 we have what we see today – a wonderful centre for people to visit and enjoy the days of yore and the Suffolk Punch. Highly recommended!

St Edmund's statue, Bury St Edmunds

This statue, represents a milestone in Suffolk history, and is situated in the Cathedral and Abbey Gardens, Bury St Edmunds. St Edmund is the patron saint of both Suffolk and Norfolk and, at one time, patron saint of England before St George. It is a known fact that many people from both counties still feel he should be our national patron saint, and for very good reasons!

But that's not the reason why he stands there today. The plaque beneath the statue reads,

The sculpture by Elizabeth Frink CBE
Commissioned by West Suffolk County Council
to mark the end of its administration of the area of the ancient liberty of St Edmund
upon the establishment of the Suffolk County Council in 1974.
Elizabeth Frink was born in Thurlow
The sculpture was unveiled by the Earl of Stradbroke Lord Lieutenant of Suffolk
17th July 1976

(The Windmill House Collection)

Up to 1974, there were two separate counties, West Suffolk, governed from Bury St Edmunds, and East Suffolk, governed from Ipswich. They merged together and Suffolk, as we know it today, was born.

The rivalry between these two counties seems to have disappeared and we have a united Suffolk. Perhaps we ought to have a united East Anglia with Suffolk and Norfolk merging as one? I think I know what the answer to that would be – No!

The Haverhill roundabout

This is the world's first roundabout to contain a sculpture lit by laser and blue sodium lights, and is known as *The Spirit of Enterprise*. It was designed by Rob Olins and erected on what is known as the Gateway roundabout. Some say that it represents enterprise taking a tumble. *Howsumever*, it is unique and takes a bit of getting used to, especially during the day. But at night, it really does look good.

Maggie Hambling, however, is famously quoted as saying, that if it's not controversial, it's not worth doing. This sculpture was therefore worth doing.

(The Windmill House Collection)

West Stow Anglo-Saxon village

This is a must for me. I have written four books on Suffolk now, and I have waxed lyrical about our Anglo-Saxon heritage: how it's affected our surnames, our place-names, our character, our humour, our everything. This village is on the original site of an Anglo-Saxon settlement dating back to AD 420, over 1,500 years ago. There's a wealth of our ancestry here, and perhaps explains why Suffolk is so Suffolk. It makes an ideal day out and you will be surprised to find that some things haven't changed all that much neither – the plough for a start!

(By kind permission of St Edmundsbury Borough Council, Heritage Service)

(By kind permission of
Gainsborough's House Trust)

Gainsborough's House, Sudbury

I've covered this somewhat in the chapter 'Famous Owd Suffolkers'. I will reiterate, though, that if it wasn't for the hard work and dedication of all the people and staff associated with Gainsborough's House throughout its history, then a great many Gainsborough masterpieces would have left the country and ended up abroad. Thank you Gainsborough's House, most sincerely, in keeping this world-famous Suffolk artist alive in Suffolk.

(The Windmill House Collection)

Adastral Park, Martlesham

In 1968, on the flat lands of East Suffolk, a great man-made structure would suddenly dominate the skyline – Adastral Park – housing British Telecom's science and research centre.

Yes, it brought welcome employment to the area and ,yes, many discoveries have been made to benefit mankind but, this gigantic structure (gigantic for Suffolk, that is), does have its critics. I suppose, though, we have to take a balanced view but the caption is very poignant!

Southwold beach huts

I suppose these beach huts have become iconic and create a colourful feature on the Suffolk coastline. Most are well kept and maintained, with only the odd one here and there needing a lick of paint. Some of the huts are just numbered but, generally speaking, we have some wonderful and creative names above the door; some very humorous. It makes Southwold look a happy place, even on a dull rainy day. *Howsumever*, if you want to buy one, then you need to put your hand in your pocket a long, long way down, as the caption indicates.

(The Windmill House Collection)

(By kind permission of St Edmundsbury Borough Council, Heritage Service)

Moyse's Hall, Bury St Edmunds

If you want to find out about the history of West Suffolk, from prehistoric times to the present day, then go no further than Moyse's Hall Museum in Bury St Edmunds. It is a very fitting place to have a museum – why?

Moyse's Hall, (don't forget the apostrophe!), has overlooked Bury St Edmunds' market for nigh on a thousand years, ever since it was built in 1180. It's had many usages, including being a tavern, a workhouse, warehouse, police station and from 1889, a museum.

The museum is most famous for having some gruesome items from the William Corder trial, (for the murder of Maria Marten at the Red Barn, Polstead). But it also has on display a magnificent history of West Suffolk through the ages, with some extremely varied, interesting and unique displays.

CHAPTER 9

A Duzzy Look at
a Suffolk Village

I had the great pleasure to have a meeting with two sisters representing Coddenham History Club, Mrs Sally Garrod and Mrs Sylvia Bickers. We spent an evening trawling through the archives of Coddenham, and some of our finds were both fascinating and enthralling. It was a history of Coddenham and its people over the last century and more, including a magnificent photographic collection. There were also some photos that lent *theirselves* to rather a *duzzy* eccentric slant. We really did have some fun sorting through this wonderful collection.

Sheep Shearing
(Coddenham History Society)

It's also worth noting that these two ladies married two men from Suffolk. Why is this worth noting? Both these gals come from ... Yes, you've guessed it ... Norfolk! They had to come south to find two decent blokes!

Having said all that, and joking apart, we had a wonderful evening, and from the *duzzy* look at a Suffolk village that follows, I think you'll see why.

Lady at the Well
(Coddenham History Society)

Outside the Post Office
(Coddenham History Society)

Milk Delivery Van
(Coddenham History Society)

Men Mardelling
(Coddenham History Society)

Wooden Bridge, Barham
(Coddenham History Society)

Outside The Duke's Head
(Coddenham History Society)

(Coddenham History Society)

The End